DATE DUE	
JUL 2 8 1995	
AUG 0 5 2000	
JUN 1 8 2002	
APR 0 4 2003 8/10/06	

GAYLORD   PRINTED IN U.S.A.

1170722

DAYDREAM HOUSES
OF LOS ANGELES

CHARLES JENCKS

RIZZOLI

To John Beach and John Chase for the many happy hours spent LA house-chasing

Back cover
Yellow House - The Archetypal Daydream, painting by Roland E. Coate, 1976. (Renée Missal)

Published in the United States of America in 1978 by
RIZZOLI INTERNATIONAL PUBLICATIONS, INC.
712 Fifth Avenue/New York 10019

Library of Congress Catalog Card Number: 78-57904

ISBN: 0-8478-0177-2

Printed and bound in Hong Kong

CONTENTS

Figures refer to illustration numbers

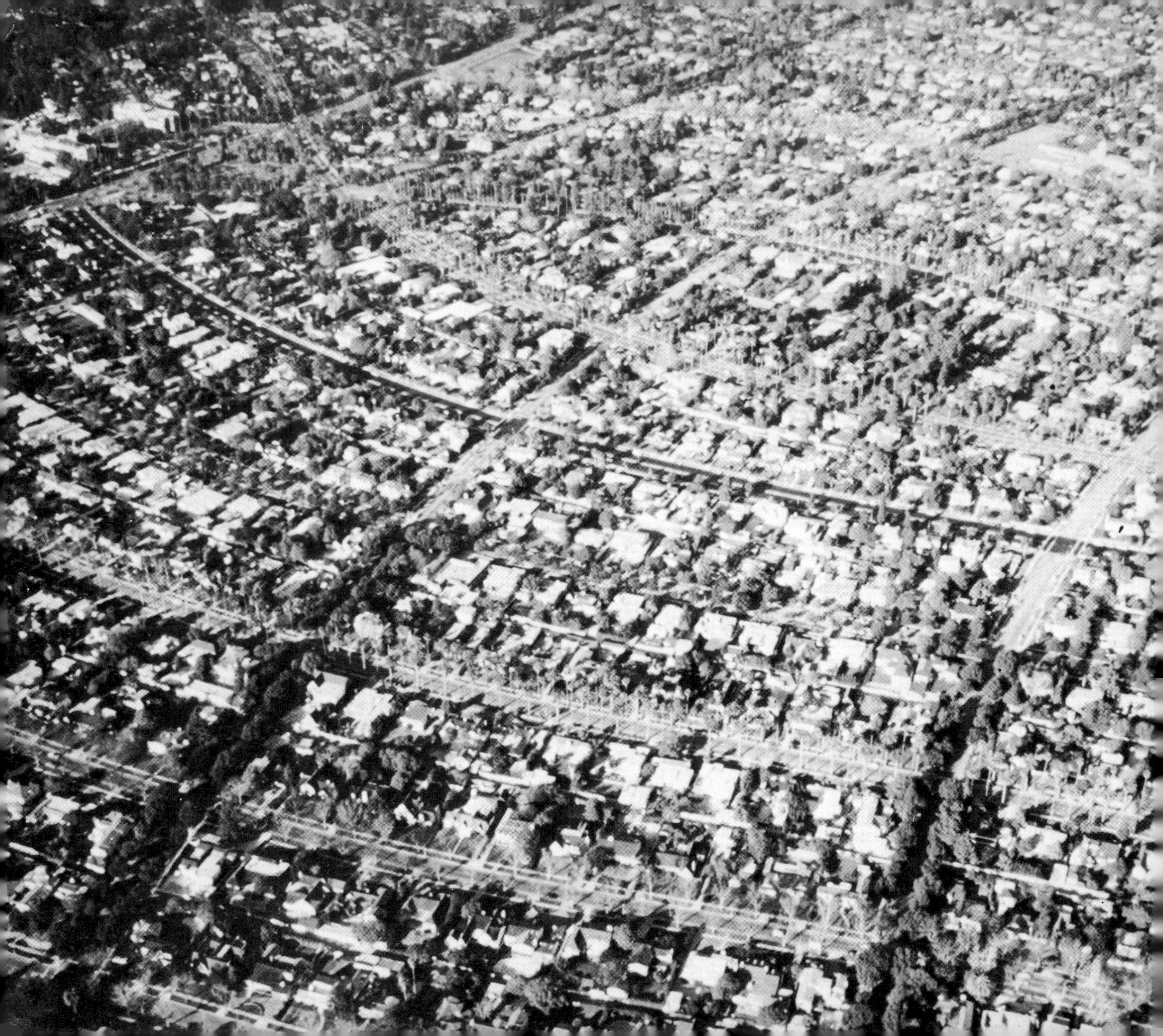

INTRODUCTION

A natural, first response to the exaggerated houses of Los Angeles is one of despair. They display obvious — much too obvious — signs of snobbery, status-seeking and kitsch; they mix motifs pillaged from every known style, combine them in an ungrammatical way and are brazen enough to do this with explicitly shoddy material. All these faults I would grant immediately; indeed even the revulsion with kitsch and excessive display. This, it seems to me, is an inevitable, even necessary, part of one's response to these houses, but it's a revulsion tempered by other feelings, those of attraction and amusement, the delight or shock in seeing custom broken. In fact, because of the strong contradictory feelings they evoke (a result of their exaggerated qualities) it is particularly hard to give them an appropriate and modest appreciation.

The Daydream Houses, to give a portmanteau label to these diverse confections, have been mostly built or modified in the last fifteen years, at a time when houses were becoming more and more standardised. Whereas nineteenth century house building was an opportunity for architectural expression, and individual expression as well, this hasn't been the case very often in the twentieth century. One can't find whole districts created today comparable with the hills of San Francisco or the suburbs of Antwerp, where each house is not only different from the next but amusing and idiosyncratic as well. One can't drive around new towns responding to personal variation. This is a pity, because architecture should be an expressive art form and one which is, if not as elevated and rich as art, at least as responsive and colourful as clothing. On this score some districts of Los Angeles rate very highly, as does the boathouse community of Sausalito Bay, one of the few areas where house-watching is an enjoyable sport.

A drive around West Hollywood, 'Boys Town', or 'Mount Olympus', or even Beverly Hills is a ritualised pastime with its own rules and acquired pleasures. I don't mean movie star home gazing, which has resulted in regular bus tours since 1922, but a more peculiar and developed taste. It may be a taste for architecture that has become completely vegetative (or almost so, 22) a taste for doors that grow bigger than walls (42, 43), a taste for the incongruous juxtaposition and the ludicrous botch (mansard roof surprised by *oeil-de-boeuf,* 34) and an eye for subtle distinctions (astroturf blended with real grass, 20). But to really enjoy the urban mixture or to watch the way one house comments on another or develops a

◁ THE BEVERLY HILLS ENVIRONMENT, with tree-lined curving roads, swimming pools, tennis courts and all the *luxe, calme et volupté* which fertiliser and money can bring to the desert.

theme one has to evolve a skill at *naming* new hybrids. This game, at best a competition between two or three players, can occupy an afternoon of driving. Some of the results are used here in naming the conglomerate beasts — 'Spreadwing Cadillac', 'Ronchamp Ski-jump with Mushroom Overtones', 'Topiary Fascist'. As one can see from the labels, which are sardonic like most response to kitsch, the designers have gone on a stylistic holiday and combined genres which are usually given separate sleeping arrangements. Indeed styles cohabit almost at random, with permissive coupling that may look more like a multi-ethnic orgy than a simple case of intermarriage.

Even whole categories of buildings carry this hybrid aspect: 'Neo-Class' is a mixture of 'New Class' and 'Pseudo-Classical'. The eight categories of houses come from naming games and thus shouldn't be taken as the last word in scholarly classification. Some pigeon-holes are distinct and have been so for forty years; for instance the 'Witches' Houses' variously called 'Ann-Hathaway-Cottage', 'Hansel and Gretel', or 'Haunted Gnomic' (52-59). You can always spot this kind of fantasy by the pointed eaves, undulating roofs and quaint windows, because the average Witch House has been standardised and mass-produced since the thirties. But even this obvious, clear category can be transformed into exotic hybrids which may be Oriental or Japanese in flavour (57). The type which starts in 1925 with the Spadina House in Beverly Hills, designed by Oliver Hill, mutates through several films into thatched gnome cottages (where the children of movie-stars played while their parents traded recollections) and then ultimately leads to the haunted apartment house, the 'witch communes'.

Two categories of Daydream Houses, 'Boys Town Variegated' and 'Beverly Hills Variegated' make no stylistic distinctions but are based entirely on location, because, it seems to me, the areas as a whole are more important than individual formal differences. Some categories such as 'LA Door' come from the accentuation of a single feature — in this case the entrance which is usually inflated in size as well as ornamental importance. 'LA Door' is not exclusive to Los Angeles, I have seen several such marvels in Houston, but its characteristic habitat is this sprawling city, telling us, I suppose, something about the way people like to welcome their guests and show off their edifice to the speeding motorist. They have an obvious parallel with billboards, fireplaces, and the radiator of a Rolls Royce (40-45).

'Span Miss' is related to Spanish Mission Revival but, according to the horrible pun latent in its appellation, a near miss and rather like span (an architectural verb, similar to cooking fat). For reasons which escape me Span Miss has incorporated Modern Parabolic, those parabolic forms characteristic of Almost-Modernism. It's one of the most popular styles because of the Spanish vernacular revival and because such movie stars as Valentino once favoured it. The other favoured styles such as Olde English, American Colonial and French Provincial are not treated here because although they are the reigning modes their fantasy does not reach the height even of a daydream. Rather they are the conventional signs of middle America, fastidiousness plus conformity. By contrast the Daydream Houses have a notional fantasy about them, similar to a momentary reverie. 'That Louis XIV detail I saw would look kind of nice in blue and white stucco and, since he was a great eater, why not have some food in the pediment... uh, lobsters' (5). Such trains of thought, such fancy as opposed to imagination, are characteristic of daydreams and the lighter type of mental activity — doggerel, puns, farce, whimsy and pastiche. All these are undoubtedly minor art forms, but should not be dismissed because of their modesty — or rather false modesty. They may not be the full blown, serious dream house — the Brighton Pavilion, the Villa Rotunda — but they may nevertheless provide lessons for current architecture, which has all too often denied itself the pleasures of elaboration and is much too self-important to let itself be, intentionally, funny.

A word should be said about Movie Star houses since they constitute such a recognisable type, and one that has been well observed by architectural lovers, and others, since the twenties. The Mayor of Beverly Hills in 1926, Will Rogers, said 'my most important job as mayor is directing folks to Mary Pickford's house', an onerous duty which has now been thankfully spread over many shoulders, including those of bus guides and map sellers.

Mary Pickford and Douglas Fairbanks were 'the Royal Family of America' who lived, most democratically, in 'Pickfair' — inevitably called the 'White House of Hollywood'. The commonplace metaphor is still the same: movie stars are a kind of democratic royalty, freely elected by American moviegoers, and encompassing a plurality of backgrounds rather than a single dynastic family. One *Guide and Map to Movie & TV Star Homes* put the mixed, and mixed up, metaphor this way:

> If we are a nation of reigning stars, then these many palaces and showplaces reflect the status and tastes of the American Royalty and is as much a part of our culture as the stone buildings of government in Washington D.C.

The first point to be accepted is that, in spite of appearances, these houses aren't inexpensive. In fact the hills of Beverly and Bel Air are probably the richest in the world including those filled with real gold or oil. If, say, 20,000 people live in them, fairly closely packed, and the houses sell from $100,000 to $3.5 million, you get a total figure that is way beyond my desk calculator. According to a real estate specialist, who lives in the beautiful 'Hedge House' (22), the average Beverly Hills house sells for over half a million and the cost is rising steadily. People are moving every five years and a game of 'musical houses', as she put it, keeps the market rising. Most occupants are not celebrities but, if an indentifiable group, are doctors. The reason people move here, she averred, was the excellent school system and the great community spirit (the mutual aid of concerned housewives which approached the ideal of a medieval commune).

The oscillation in taste, and therefore real estate value, followed some fairly discernible trends. In the sixties, Mediterranean style was in, whereas recently it was English Tudor. In the fifties Spanish Mission was converted to Modern style by squaring off the arches. Now that Modern and Craig Ellwood are no longer fashionable, people are filling in their rectangular arcades and making them round again — 'they like things that are authentic' she explained. True Modern is now very rare except for a variant known as 'Hawaiian Modern' which means large overhangs in thatch. Her own house was Modern covered up by fast growing camouflage and I saw one glass and steel Ellwood that had been converted to classical, with thick Corinthian columns taking the place of etiolated I-beams.

As a type the Movie Star House displays two very definite aspects: power, as signified in a massive and conventionally bland front (like a provincial city hall) and a rambling, spread out informality (like a relaxed Texan with his boots off and his limbs spread akimbo over sofa, stool and coffee table). The homes come in five standard styles, but nearly all display these two qualities. Informality lets the constant stream of variable guests feel 'at home' even though their backgrounds are inevitably different; and power gives a proper sense of propriety and good standing to these 'public' figures. The signs of power of course enhance the means of control — the guard dogs, electronic gates, television cameras, and alarm systems that surround the house. These have reached Mannerist and manic proportions since the Manson murders, and so Star watching can be a rather hazardous pastime if you get too close. Guard dogs trained to eat first and bark later, spikes which sprock out of the ground, signs warning 'Severe Tire Damage' (of course these appear all over LA) — perhaps laser beams shoot between the two Palladian gate posts, such is the fantasy induced by the signs and weapons. And yet these houses must, at the same time, be welcoming. They are built to be seen, ogled at, emulated — the main point of stardom. So quite an elaborate mixture of signs is produced, half of them inviting the prying eye, the other half saying *keep out*.

The Average Star House has two large, indeed oversized, gate posts, the automated swing gates, several warning signs about children and German shepherds, a two-way radio system to speak into, a short curving drive signifying Country Estate, two cars parked near the entrance (preferably a Mercedes convertible and a $52,000 Stutz with acronymic licence plates, bearing the actors initials) carefully manicured ivy (that is watered nightly by jet sprays concealed in the ivy with the alarm system); oaks, palms, hydrangeas, bougainvillaeas and jacarandas abound, and peering out from all this lush exotica is a discrete swath of roof line and a grand entry porch. The cars and planting are as important as the house and usually more interesting. Indeed architecturally the stars' houses are timid and reticent, 'unobtrusive in the extreme' as one Starologist termed it. They suffer a kind of architectural deprivation so complete that it should be disallowed by law even for the very rich.

The layout and functions of the Average Star House are more interesting although equally standard. Near the entry hall are spacious rooms, everything you'd find in a grand suburban home including den, bar and library. But then, further back come the more exotic chambers — a lanai with open bar sculpted towards the swimming pool, a tennis court, which is now more coveted than the pool, some place for the children to play like a Gnome's House, and finally the all important Shrine Room, a styled up American game room. This often occupies a pavilion detached from the house, and it contains a mixture of activities for our well-rounded star — billiards, stereo, computer pin ball, an exercise bicycle, fifty signed portraits of other celebrities including two of the Shah, trophies, Oscars, and the whole point of this Shrine Room, the projection equipment. At the press of a button Post-Impressionists slide aside, a screen descends and one watches Reg Butler walk out on Scarlett O'Hara for the thirteenth time. Every star's house has some equivalent to this screen room-rumpus room, where past triumphs are relived and the golden memories are kept alive. They bear some iconographic relation to the cemetery at Forest Lawn and the Movieland Wax Museum, being a quintessential attempt at earthly immortality. Many Shrine Rooms remain posthumously just as the star left them to settle for the last time in Forest Lawn.

Exceptions to the above norm of *unobtrusivius in extremis* are the houses of James Coburn, Gypsy Rose Lee, Jayne Mansfield, Jennifer Jones, Bernie Kovacs, the old mansions such as Grayhall and Green Acres, Hugh Hefner's Playboy Mansion West, and of course Liberace's house (or one of seven of them, 20-21). Liberace is undoubtedly the democratic King of showmanship and the only royal to take his public role of celebrification utterly seriously, with every part of his house styled up. Various modes are practised, of which Late Baroque Pianoism is the greatest. Like the designers of Boys Town he plays with architectural motifs, and even if it isn't the High Game of serious architecture, it is nonetheless a form of enjoyment, erotic in its self-obsession.

If poetry is unrequited love, then architecture is a species of sexual fetishism. All architecture has its erogenous zones and secret places of pleasure. Doors and windows are exaggerated at Boys Town just as breasts and buttocks are larger than is functionally necessary. Parts of a building stick out from the main body catching the eye of a passer-by like the billowing skirt of a young girl. The architects, or interior designers who went exterior, planned this. They elaborated the pleasure centres with strong colours, voluptuous planting around the entrance, and extra smooth surface more-silky-than-skin (as is leather and vinyl). Invariably certain parts of the house are hidden, or rather half-revealed like the leg through a diaphanous skirt. Suggestive veiling of the belly dancer finds its counterpart in architectural striptease, where expectations are aroused by showing only half the eye-catcher.

One can glimpse the living room through the haze of a trellis or curtain, a statue behind the hedge — there is always a promise of more to come. The titillation, as in Mae West, rests entirely on being explicit about coming attractions while, at the same time, witholding gratification and sending the whole game up. The architecture of Boys Town is perfectly frank about a natural love of form — pilasters, fluted columns, mouldings, all the articulae which mould light and shade — and reveals this healthy fetish as Mae West might display her lower thigh, but then hides the rest away from the prying eye and leaves it for the private realm, the frequent guest, the old friend.

As in fetishism it's a case of *pars pro toto,* the part taking over command from the whole, especially in the converted bungalows where the last ten feet of stuck-on façade mask the reality of the thirty foot stucco behind. These 'bungaloids' (as they're known) used to be modest cottages, or servant quarters for the rich of nearby Beverly Hills, but now their style has changed from something vaguely Spanish to something vaguely else as the interior decorators distort the language which they elsewhere use straight for their clients.

This distortion is inevitably towards exaggeration, towards the supersign. Like the shiny black rubber suit which is a condensed sign of skin (more homogeneous, smooth and squashy than the real thing) these forms are distilled versions of their normal counterparts. They exaggerate just the relevant qualities we find appealing: size, contrast in texture and colour, ornament, repetitive pattern, lushness. The bungaloid will over-articulate all the orifices — the windows, doors, chimneys, mail slots — and all the protuberances which can be fondled — the doorknockers, handles, balustrades and carriage lamps. This is fine and just as it should be: all architecture heightens some parts of its structure over others. The Gothic church makes a fetish of its entrance façade and towers, the Renaissance palazzo heightens its street façade — both building types dramatise the public and visible fronts in quite explicit opposition to their private behinds. Alberti's Palazzo Rucelli, the first of a type, is as much billboard as his Santa Maria Novella façade. Of course they are more than billboards but they are also these, a fact which is generally obscured in orthodox architectural history. If architecture is an art, then like all art it must call attention to its expressive plane of meaning and this entails an over-concentration on formal, or tactile, or perceivable matter.

To object to this architectural fetishism would be like objecting to lipstick, earrings and décolletage. Breasts and buttocks and etc. are here to be enjoyed just as are pediments and architraves and, as sexologists are now emphasising, making fetishes of these parts in small degree is not only natural to everyone but positively desirable — a sign, a stimulus of a more generalised sexuality to come.

For this very reason of course one could object to the exaggerated details of Boys Town: they do not ordinarily lead to greater pleasures but remain like the reductive fetish, the boot, as a substitute for larger concerns. The daydream doesn't become a dream, the life-style a way of life, or the façade a convincing introduction to an equally grand space. Unlike the church façade which is a prelude to even greater attractions, the part has taken over completely from the whole.

Nonetheless, unlike puritanical building, there is a recognition and acceptance of basic architectural passion. The proper or appropriate elements are fetishized, the doors and windows and not just the utilitarian elements such as plumbing and structure. It's a question of ritual and social meaning, the fact that daily life and such social discourse as entertaining friends, entering and leaving, should be marked and supported by architecture.

A few *bona fide* architects such as Frank Lloyd Wright and John Lautner acknowledge this aspect in their work, and they have also produced whimsical, metaphorical buildings in LA. The 'Hollyhock House' and 'Chemosphere House' respectively were both designed around a fanciful image that is rather appliquéd onto the building. In the former a flower becomes the excuse for some startling and repetitive ornament, in the latter a flying saucer is the design conceit, but since neither image is taken very seriously by the architect they *do* qualify as acceptable daydreams. Most of their remaining architecture is too good to be included in this book (although Wright's Ennis House and Lautner's 'Salad Bowl' pass the test).

The question of how we judge daydreams thus becomes pressing, how we separate the good from the bad, the creative from the hackneyed, or from the whole genre of convincing dream houses. Clearly they occupy a certain historical and critical position somewhere between serious architecture done well — and very, very Low Pseud. Since we don't give this middling category much thought but consign it to a kind of critical limbo of silence, it escapes perception, or rather is perceived wildly one way or the other — over-praised or over-condemned. It's instructive to compare our reactions to those of the 1880s when the carpenter-built houses of San Francisco were emerging and the 'Queen Anne Style' was in vogue. East Coast critics from the *New York Times* were horrified by what they saw ('not a sober house') and Montgomery Schuyler, the leading critic, could condemn the supporters of this hybrid style as 'a frantic and vociferous mob, who welcome the "new departure" as the disestablishment of all standards, whether of authority or of reason, and as an emancipation from all restraints, even those of public decency.' This over-reaction is typical. It's true that the 'Queen Anne' houses lacked urban propriety and broke formal grammar, but they were often direct responses to individual expression. In that sense they were more appropriate to the city than much dull architecture which, because of its dullness, escaped censure.

Daydream Houses also have an immediate, sensual quality, an ability to make you turn your head away from the traffic, look and, however reluctantly, smile.

A note on touring

The approximate location of the houses is shown on the diagrammatic map. The basic areas for architectural delectation are:

1 Beverly Hills, following the spine of Sunset Boulevard. There are Movie Star maps for this, but alas, ninety-five per cent of the houses are not even at the daydream level.

2 West Hollywood between Robertson Boulevard and Doheny Drive has the greatest concentration of amusing and creative remodels.

3 The Mount Olympus development off Laurel Canyon has some rather high Schlock Classicism.

4 Mulholland Drive and the 'Dona' streets (Dona Alicia etc) have the same plus some John Lautner and Frank Lloyd Wright buildings.

5 The area around Beverly Boulevard and Larchmont Boulevard contains amusing remodels.

6 Two Daydream Houses of Frank Lloyd Wright are located near Griffith Park.

Individual examples can be found all over LA in areas like Culver City, Trusdale Estates and the film lots such as Twentieth Century Fox. Unfortunately because this book was written and produced in London not all the house locations could be checked, and in some cases addresses are approximate as indicated.

The author and publisher would welcome any additional information and corrections. A sequel edition is being planned — *'More Daydream Houses of Los Angeles'*. If you have a good slide of a house you think might qualify, send it with a title, description and address to Academy Editions, 7 Holland Street London W8, England. Unfortunately material cannot be returned, but due credits will be given.

THE PLATES

1 VAUX-LE-VICOMTE AT FIFTEEN FEET, 8937 Ashcroft Avenue. Note the Second Empire lighting, the LA Door and topiary petrol pumps.

2 YELLOW FACE HOUSE WITH PURPLE LIPSTICK, 9003 Norma. Planting is always a sign of protection and status. Note the bungalow to the right, the 1930 standard which is everywhere remodelled in Boys Town.

3 BLACK FACE HOUSE WITH MORTUARY OVERTONES, 8836 Rangley Avenue. Note the rusticated base, the truncated ped, cut-off windows and Forest Lawn detailing.

4 IRONIC IONIC WITH CHISELLED CORNER, 8960 Cynthia Street. To some this looks like a municipal water-tank, to others like a Toy Town Hall.

5 BABY BLUE LOBSTER WITH CORNER FROSTINGS, 8834 Dorrington Avenue. Vaguely Federal with ungainly proportions of ped and pilasts carefully calculated.

6 UPTIGHT CLASSICIST WITH LA DOOR, 8827 Dorrington Avenue. The Rolls Royce and fireplace overtones mix with Regency and billboard.

7 EYESHADOW BOX WITH LANVIN EDGING, 8980 Lloyd Place. It could be Balmain but it's definitely in the cosmetic ine; the cleanliness inspires emulation.

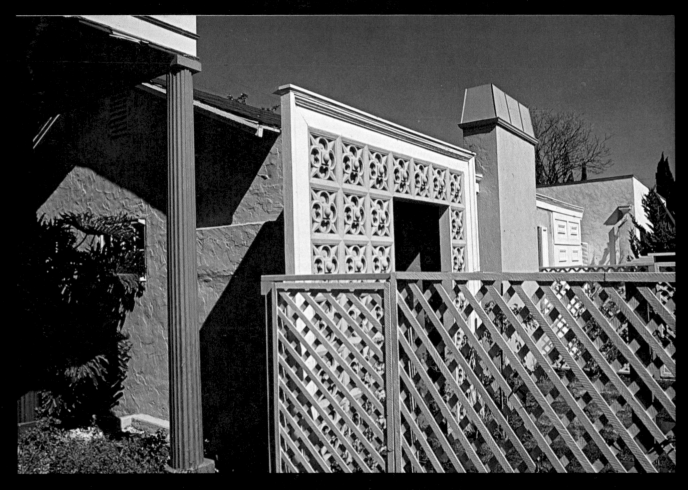

8 TRELLIS SCREEN GOTHIC, 8967 Norma. Trefoils, mansardic chimney and Op Art effects in baby blue-grey billboard.

9 PICTURE FRAME CLASSICAL WITH EGYPTIAN CARDBOARD, 8986 Norma. The front and sides are in masterful disjunction as are the brick podium and letter-box.

10 JAPANESE CARP WITH SHIPPING CONTAINER, 8953 Dick Street. A flamboyant cypress marks the meeting of East and Western batten board. Note the discreet colouring and carriage lamp.

11 EGYPTIAN FAN WITH SPECKLE BRICK, Ashcroft Avenue. Again the billboard of trellis and planting to gain a few more feet of privacy.

12 MEXICAN CAFE WITH BURNT OUT LOOK, 9015 Dick Street. Speckle brick, lazy palm and 'real' antiqued this 'Casa del Leone'.

13 STEPPED EDGE PUEBLO PALLADIAN WITH LA DOOR, 9051 Lloyd Place. Note the grand stairway and future cypresses. The house was being refurbished when photographed.

14 HARRODS CUPBOARD WITH LA DOOR AND CARRIAGE LAMP, 8907 Rosewood Avenue, 1973. Boys Town architecture is often as fast-changing and responsive as clothing.

15 HARRODS CUPBOARD WITH WEDGEWOOD SCREENS, 1977. When architects talk of personalisation, do-it-yourself and popular self-build they usually have something else in mind.

16 DEBBIE REYNOLDS EGYPTOID WITH CIRCUS TENT AND CAR DISPLAY, 813 Greenway Drive. The house changes every few years. Three replicars are displayed in the garage off right.

17 ZSA ZSA CASTELLATED, 1001 Bel Air Road. I'm not sure about the windows or materials, but Zsa Zsa, married more than once, is known as the 'greatest house-keeper in Hollywood'.

18 KIRK DOUGLAS — A LESSER SPLASH WITH TENNIS COURT AND LANAI, 707 N. Cannon Drive. The house, on sale for five years at $725,000 is classified by real estate specialists as 'Two-Storey Traditional'.

19 HENRY FONDA — NAMELESS MEDITERRANEAN, 10744 Chalon Road, Bel Air. The authentic Spanish style with pantiles was popularised by Valentino, and the neo-vernacular of California.

20 LIBERACE ASTROTURF — WITH OUTDOOR HEATERS AND REAL CYPRESSES, 8433 Harold Way. Many celebrities have tents, awning and *porte-cochères* as if their house were a Sultan's hotel.

21 LIBERACE AT HOME STYLE, 8433 Harold Way. The only room without a surfeit of Late Baroque Pianoism.

22 HEDGE HOUSE WITH HIGHWAY TRIM AND TOPIARY ENTRANCE, 802 Crescent Drive. Originally Modern style which later owners decided to camouflage except for the entablature — which is nicely echoed by the hedge.

23 TELESCOPED ART DECO WITH SPAN MISS OVERTONES, 282 Mapleton Drive. Stained glass window and a variety of window shapes contrast with the large arch and rectangle.

24 PREDATORY MANSARD WITH LA DOOR, 130 Mapleton Drive. Note the lighting fixtures, excessive rustication, *oeil-de-boeuf* and elongated proportions.

25 WEDGEWOOD MANSARD WITH ALL POSSIBLE SYMBOLS, 333 Copa de Oro. The electronic gates, urns, cypresses, finials, lighting standards, paving, fountain, LA door are all greater than the sum of the parts. The house belongs to TV sportscaster Phyllis George.

26 BRANCH BANK PARTHENON, 7979 Mulholland Drive. A popular style for houses, drive-in banks and the All American Hamburger chain.

27 TOPIARY FASCIST, 8039 Mulholland Drive. Nature abundant and in chains. Planting surrounds all LA houses and

28 BELVEDERE HELLO WITH MANICURED VERDURE, N. Hercules Drive, 'Mount Olympus.' Architraves tend to be streamlined, doors tend to be Baroque, planting variegated.

29 BELVEDERE HELLO WITH SPOT-LIT WEEPER, N. Hercules Drive. The embracing portico lets you know you have arrived. Most houses on 'Mount Olympus' are 'Neo Class'.

30 SPREADWING CADILLAC WITH LA DOOR AND HENRY MOORISH, 2450 N. Hercules Drive. A surreal mixture of automobile and art imagery with excessively blank windows; the house to the left is almost as zoorck.

31 DE CHIRICO AUBERGINE WITH WOOD GRAIN AND POWER LINES, 3311 Dona Rosa. Behind the rustic wood a swimming pool? Off left a power station. Note the arcade extended and opened to frame the view.

32 LOGGIA MODERN WITH UNGRAMMATICAL IONIC, 2110 Hercules. Note the Mexican door and lighting fixtures. Alberti warned architects not to mix columns and flat arcades.

33 TENNIS SKIRT BATTEN BOARD WITH FINIALS, 570 Plymouth Boulevard? Wood slats pick up the diagonal of the bungalow roof; topiary and bulbous light are also masterful touches.

4 SURPRISED OY-DA-BUFFALO WITH TYROLEAN HAT, 147 South Lucerne. The ultimate ingénue tack-on with
rustic shingle and brick, real grass imitating astroturf, the LA door and unbelievable proportions.

35 LATE CHARLES ADAMS WITH WHITE PLEATS, 225 North Gower. The bungalow extension even swings out welcoming the car. The remorseless blackness of this black is not unintentional.

36 COPPER COATED MANSARDIC WITH CORNER HAPPENINGS, 571 Windsor Boulevard. Again the notional *porte-cochère* divides the new attachment from the old bungalow.

37 ENCHANTED VIEW WITH DISPLACED MANSARD, 2431 —? Many apartment communities have taken over th

38 MANSARDIC OVER INTERNATIONAL STYLE WITH PORTCULLIS, near Paramount Studios. A very flat, cool and symmetrical drive-in court contrasts with the lush planting and decorative fascia.

89 MANSARDIC ROW FILM SET HOUSING, Twentieth Century Fox Studios. A movie set used also for offices mimic

40 LA DOOR WITH MANSARDIC AND ELECTRONIC REGENCY, 3323 Dona Rosa. Asymmetrical, International Style

41 CHINESE I DON'T KNOW WHY WITH DOMINO DOOR, near Hedges Place? The blue colour and patterned motifs are quite restful.

42 BIG DOOR, 8976 Lloyd Place. Batten boards on this false front in Boys Town. Some day there may be a house which is all door.

43 BIGGER DOOR, 326 Lapeer Street. Often the blank, off-white wall serves as a backdrop for shadows or planting.

44 RUSTIC DOOR, 9019 Norma. Typical watered-desert planting. The door that breaks the roof line is also normal.

5 FASTIDIOUS DOOR. 9046 Vista Grande Street. Another Boys Town false front, and in the colours of a French château

46 SPAN MISS WITH PARABOLIC MODERN AND STAINED GLASS, 1830 Outpost. The truncated tower and Monterey porch (?) look almost authentic. Why many living rooms in this style have parabolic windows escapes me.

7 PARABOLIC EYEBROW TACK-ON, near Robert Burns Park? The false front provides a nice transition to the private realm.

48 MISSION STYLE LIGHTHOUSE WITH BELVEDERE HELLO, circa 3100 Glendower. The incompleteness of circle and tower seem to be carefully calculated.

9 RONCHAMP SKI-JUMP WITH MUSHROOM OVERTONES, 8968 Dick Street. The ultimate bungaloid face-lift with erotic curves, picturesque windows and movie star awning. The tiny bell tower by the entrance provides the perfect balance.

50 WEDGEWOOD MISSION WITH CHRISTMAS BELLS, 4307 Avocado Street? Awnings, fringes, poplars and ventilators in counterpoint.

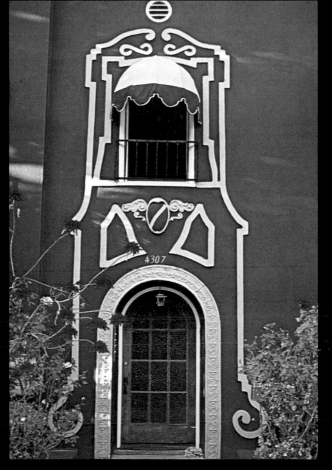

WEDGEWOOD MISSION ENTRANCE. Baroque strapwork (?) accentuates the speaker's (?) porch

52 SPADINA WITCHES HOUSE WITH BROOMSTICK TENSION BAR, Carmelita Avenue. Designed in 1925 as the Story book House by Oliver Hill, for screenwriter Hans Kraley, so that he could 'recall' his Normandy days; note the quaint shutters.

53 WITCHES NORMANDY WITH RIPPLE ROOF, near Rosewood Avenue. The rounded roof edges, pointed eaves and asymmetry are all standard.

54 WITCHES TUDOR WITH DISTORTED WINDOWS, circa 2700 Glendower. Note the sinister snaking timbers and creepy, upturned roof.

55 HANSEL AND GRETEL WITH ROUNDED ROOF CORNERS, on Avocado Street. Planting punctuates the white background.

56 HARD-TIMES WITCH WITH MARBLEIZED SHINGLE, near Van Ness Avenue. The charm of squat proportions and impossible materials.

57 JAPANESE WITCH WITH PLASTIC SNOW SHINGLE, near Griffith Park. A curved entry hedge to the right leads to a diminutive fountain and gargantuan brackets.

58 ANN HATHAWAY VILLAGE, 4350 Beverly Boulevard. The enclosed courtyard apartment group is common in LA — all the styles are represented.

59 WITCHES COMMUNE WITH RIPPLE ROOF AND ROLLED CORNERS, near Maplewood Avenue. Black and white architecture and even the black is clean.

60 FRANK LLOYD WRIGHT HOLLYHOCK HOUSE WITH MAYAN TOMB LOOK, Barnsdale Park, 1917-1920. The long, low entry way is to the left, the music and library rooms to the right and the stylised hollyhock flower is everywhere.

61 LLOYD WRIGHT MONSTER FACE HOUSE WITH TOO MANY TEETH, 5121 Franklin Avenue, 1926. Extreme contrasts: blue bathroom *vs.* pink stucco *vs.* rough concrete *vs.* green mullions. Lloyd is Frank's son.

62 JOHN LAUTNER SALAD BOWL WITH BRIDGE GIRDER, Carling House, Pacific View Drive, 1950? The industrial materials, stepped back and distorted, are used with a compositional freedom.

63 FRANK LLOYD WRIGHT AZTEC SACRIFICIAL, Ennis House, Glendower Avenue, 1924. The small ornamental concrete block is staged on horizontal, sliding layers above a cliff of artificially aided verdure. (Photo Architectural Association).

64 TWENTIETH CENTURY FOX FANTASY STREET, 20th Century Fox Studios. Stagesets, some of them used as offices, in Georgian, FLW, Schindler and variegated.